PSYCHIATRISTS

THERAPY

BOOK

A comprehensive guide on mental health, mindful Solution, prevention, management, healing conversations, counseling, techniques interventions and addiction remedy

Brandon Oliver

TABLE OF CONTENTS

CHAPTER 5   67

PSYCHOTIC DISORDERS   67

CHAPTER 6   91

COGNITIVE-BEHAVIORAL THERAPY (CBT)   91

INTRODUCTION

This compelling and insightful guide, penned by expert, transcends the traditional boundaries of self-help literature.

In this comprehensive volume, readers will find a great exploration of various therapeutic modalities, coupled with real-life happenings that illuminate the profound impact of psychiatry on individual lives. The book goes beyond conventional self-help prescriptions, offering a holistic perspective on mental health, resilience, and personal growth. With empathy and wisdom, the authors provide practical tools and exercises, empowering readers to navigate the intricacies of their own minds and fostering a path towards emotional well-being.

Whether you are grappling with specific mental health challenges or simply yearning for a deeper understanding of the human experience, Psychiatrist's Therapy Book is a compassionate and enlightening companion on your journey toward self-discovery and healing.

CHAPTER 1

UNDERSTANDING MENTAL HEALTH

Mental well-being encompasses our emotional, psychological, and social states, influencing our thoughts, emotions, actions, and stress management. It shapes our interpersonal relationships and decision-making processes. When disruptions arise in patterns of thinking, feeling, or behavior, causing distress or impeding functioning, a mental disorder may be present.

Defining mental health involves cultural and social considerations, with norms varying across societies. What is deemed normal in one culture may be a concern in another. Mental illness spans a spectrum of conditions affecting mood, cognition, and behavior, transitioning from occasional concerns to persistent issues causing stress and functional impairment. Roughly one in five adults experiences mental illness annually, and its onset can happen at any age.

From childhood through adulthood, mental health is crucial, influencing cognitive processes, moods, and behaviors. Treatment for mental illness depends on factors like type and severity, often involving a tailored combination of approaches. While mild cases may be managed by primary health care professionals, a collaborative team approach is often necessary to address psychiatric, medical, and social needs comprehensively.

Sadly, negative perceptions and biases toward individuals with mental health conditions persist, largely rooted in ignorance rather than factual understanding. Combating the stigma requires awareness and education.

Mental health conditions encompass a spectrum, impacting thinking, mood, and behavior. Nearly one in five adults grapple with mental illness, influenced by biological factors, life experiences, and family history. Specific conditions range from anxiety and depression to personality disorders and self-harm.

Serious Mental Illness (SMI) denotes conditions significantly hindering life and functioning. Contrary to misconceptions, having an SMI is not a choice, weakness, or flaw; it is not transient and cannot be overcome through willpower. Understanding and dispelling these misconceptions are crucial steps in fostering empathy and support for individuals dealing with serious mental illnesses.

Recognizing Early Warning Signs & Symptoms

Uncertain whether you or someone you know is grappling with mental health issues? Detecting one or more of the following feelings or behaviors may serve as an early indicator of a problem:

- Altered eating or sleeping patterns
- Withdrawal from usual activities and people
- Low or absent energy levels
- Feeling emotionally detached or indifferent
- Unexplained physical discomfort
- Sense of helplessness or hopelessness
- Increased substance use (smoking, drinking, or drugs)
- Unusual states of confusion, forgetfulness, tension, anger, distress, worry, or fear
- Conflicts and arguments with family and friends
- Significant mood swings impacting relationships

- Persistent intrusive thoughts and memories
- Auditory hallucinations or holding false beliefs
- Contemplation of self-harm or harm to others
- Inability to carry out daily tasks like caring for children or attending work or school

Guidelines for maintaining well-being with a mental health condition

Living with a mental health condition may pose challenges in various aspects of life, such as work, school, routines, relationships, social interactions, and personal care. However, with timely and consistent treatment often a blend of medication and psychotherapy it's feasible to navigate these conditions, surmount obstacles, and lead a purposeful, productive life.

Contemporary tools, evidence-based treatments, and support systems contribute to improved well-being and pursuit of personal goals. Key tips, tools, and strategies encompass:

Adhering to a treatment plan: Even if feeling better, continue therapy and medication as directed by a doctor. Collaborate with a healthcare professional to safely adjust doses or medications if necessary.

Keeping your primary care physician informed: Primary care physicians play a vital role in long-term management, particularly if also consulting with a psychiatrist.

Gaining knowledge about the condition: Being well-informed aids in adhering to the treatment plan, fostering support and understanding from loved ones.

Practicing self-care: Manage stress through activities like meditation or tai chi, maintain a healthy diet, engage in regular exercise, and ensure sufficient sleep.

Seeking support from family and friends: Maintaining relationships is crucial, and during challenging times, reaching out to loved ones for assistance can make a significant difference.

Developing coping skills: Establishing healthy coping mechanisms helps in navigating stress more effectively.

Prioritizing adequate sleep: Quality sleep enhances brain function, mood, and overall health. Consistently poor sleep is associated with conditions like anxiety and depression.

CHAPTER 2

WHAT IS PSYCHIATRY?

Psychiatry constitutes the medical discipline dedicated to investigating and addressing mental health disorders. Individuals qualified and authorized to practice this branch of medicine are referred to as psychiatrists. These professionals are capable of addressing a spectrum of mental health conditions, ranging from those affecting daily functionality, such as depression and anxiety, to those stemming from physical injuries like traumatic brain injury.

Specialized areas within psychiatry, such as addiction psychiatry, community psychiatry, child psychiatry, and social psychiatry, allow psychiatrists to focus on specific aspects of mental health. Individuals seeking therapeutic intervention may choose to consult with a psychiatrist, while others may be directed to a psychiatrist by their therapist or counselor.

Comprehending psychiatry

Psychiatry has a long history, dating back thousands of years in various forms. In ancient Greece and Rome, mental health issues were often attributed to supernatural forces until Hippocrates proposed in the 4th century B.C.E. that physiological factors might be responsible. During the Middle Ages, those with mental health conditions were typically confined to asylums, but these institutions often served more as holding facilities than actual treatment centers.

In the 18th century, French psychiatrist Philippe Pinel advocated for humane treatments for psychiatric patients, challenging the conditions in asylums. However, variations in treatment persisted well into the 20th century. In the early 20th century, psychiatrists began proposing diverse treatment approaches. While mental health conditions are now widely recognized as highly treatable, the conditions and procedures in psychiatric hospitals can still differ based on location, treated issues, and other factors.

Psychiatrists may vary in their treatment philosophies, but the fundamental belief in psychiatry is that mental health conditions have an underlying biological cause. Psychiatrists prescribe medications to address imbalances in brain chemistry contributing to mental health symptoms. While medication is a common aspect of psychiatric treatment, some psychiatrists also offer alternative interventions such as talk therapy.

When to consider a psychiatric approach

While therapy is beneficial for many individuals with mental health conditions, there are cases where therapy alone may not suffice. Conditions like depression, anxiety, PTSD, and others can be so debilitating that medications are recommended to help individuals better manage their well-being. Additionally, severe and persistent conditions like schizophrenia and bipolar disorder may, at times, necessitate medication for safety and stability. In such instances, a psychiatric approach is often suggested. While there's no one-size-fits-all solution, consulting with a qualified medical professional can help determine if psychiatry, particularly medication use, might be beneficial.

The management of medications for mental health conditions can be handled by a primary care physician or another medical provider in certain situations. However, when the condition is complex or challenging to treat, seeking the expertise of a psychiatrist is often advised. While all doctors can prescribe medications, psychiatrists are specifically trained in the treatment of mental health issues, offering a level of experience and expertise that other medical professionals may not possess.

Philosophy behind psychiatric treatment

Psychiatrists typically employ medications, sometimes in combination with other therapies, to address mental health issues. Although medications can be effective, they are not without risks, with side effects ranging from mild to severe. Moreover, the necessity of medications is not universal, as research suggests that, in many cases, antidepressants and other medications are not necessarily more effective than therapy alone.

While psychiatrists often recommend medication, individuals have the right to make their own decisions about their treatment. Psychiatrists are ethically and legally obligated to obtain informed consent, explaining the proposed treatment, potential risks, and benefits to allow individuals to make informed decisions about their participation in the treatment. Importantly, psychiatrists cannot compel individuals to undergo treatment or take medications, except in rare circumstances. Anyone seeking psychiatric care has the right to inquire about the recommended treatment and explore information about alternative treatments that may also be effective and beneficial.

What is therapy?

Therapists, counselors, shrinks, head doctors, analysts these are terms often used to describe mental health professionals. If you've watched Frasier, you likely have a basic understanding that psychologists analyze and help resolve people's problems through talk therapy, although not all psychologists host radio shows.

But what exactly is therapy, and why is it important to understand? Mental health is sometimes a sensitive topic, but having a grasp of the basics is crucial, especially if you're considering seeking treatment.

Defining Psychotherapy: Psychotherapy involves the clinical practice of alleviating emotional distress through talk therapy. Practiced by various professionals such as psychiatrists, psychologists, social workers, and licensed counselors, talk therapy delves into difficult situations, both past and present.

The Transformative Power of Therapy: Therapy is a significant step in personal development and mental health. It facilitates positive changes in self-destructive behaviors, resolves painful feelings, addresses trauma, and enhances relationships. Administered to individuals, couples, families, or groups, therapy employs diverse approaches like cognitive-behavioral therapy, psychodynamic therapy, and systems-based therapy.

Tailored Approaches in Talk Therapy: While therapists may specialize in particular modalities, they often use a combination of approaches to meet individual needs. The therapy journey, unique for each person, begins by establishing goals and next steps. Confidentiality is paramount, ensuring that both session discussions and the therapeutic process remain private.

Building a Supportive Relationship: Engaging in therapy involves creating a professional relationship with a therapist who is supportive, impartial yet on your side, and models a healthy and positive relationship experience. Experienced therapists customize mental health counseling using well-tested techniques, blending researched methods with their own perspectives based on years of practice.

Counseling vs. Psychotherapy: Although counseling and therapy are often used interchangeably, there's a distinction. Counseling is typically a short-term treatment focused on specific issues, such as addiction or domestic abuse. It emphasizes action-oriented solutions and coping skills. In contrast, psychotherapy is generally more long-term, open-ended, and explores a broader range of topics, helping individuals gain insights into patterns of thinking and behavior.

Psychologist vs. Therapist: The terms psychologist and therapist are often used interchangeably, but there are differences. Psychologists hold doctoral degrees in psychology and undergo extensive training in mental and emotional disorder evaluation and treatment. They often collaborate with psychiatrists for comprehensive patient care. Therapists, or licensed mental health counselors, possess master's degrees and offer counseling or psychotherapy, but their scope may not include all aspects of a psychologist's work.

Understanding these distinctions is crucial when considering mental health treatment, ensuring informed decisions and effective collaboration with professionals who can address individual needs.

Clinical Social Workers: Another professional in a similar vein is the clinical social worker, who holds at least a master's degree in social work and possesses the training to evaluate and treat mental illnesses. Beyond psychotherapy, social workers can offer case management, hospital discharge planning, and advocacy for patients and their families.

Who Can Benefit from Therapy?

Therapy is inclusive and does not discriminate. It caters to diverse mental health issues, with various approaches and techniques suited for individuals, couples, families, or groups. It is beneficial for overcoming challenges, ranging from deep-seated traumas to managing everyday stressors. Couples and families often use therapy to navigate relationship obstacles and enhance communication by understanding each other's patterns and behaviors. Therapy can serve as a short-term solution for specific issues or provide a platform for long-term exploration and self-discovery.

Effectiveness of Therapy: Numerous scientific studies highlight the consistently positive effects of psychotherapy across different age groups and settings, including independent practices, community centers, and hospitals. On average, clients receiving psychotherapy demonstrate more mental stability compared to 79% of clients not seeking treatment. Psychotherapy's effectiveness rivals biomedical breakthroughs, as demonstrated by Dr. Robert Rosenthal from Harvard University. While antidepressant medications remain powerful tools, their effectiveness is significantly enhanced when coupled with regular psychotherapy. Research indicates that psychotherapy is at least as effective as antidepressants during treatment and more effective in preventing symptom recurrence after treatment cessation.

Maximizing Therapy Benefits: To get the most out of therapy, the first crucial step is selecting a therapist who is the right fit. While urgency may push for quick answers, it's important to invest time in carefully choosing a therapist. Research different therapists and approaches, create a shortlist, and engage in conversations or trial sessions with each. Consider not only their credentials but also how comfortable you feel talking to them. After selecting a therapist, give the relationship at least three sessions to assess its fit.

Clearly express your needs, ask questions, and complete any recommended assignments outside of sessions. Establish outcome markers with your therapist to track positive changes and stay motivated. These markers serve as signposts, indicating progress in areas such as increased happiness, better stress management, healthier social relationships, or improved communication in the workplace. Taking an active role in your therapy process enhances its effectiveness and contributes to positive outcomes.

CHAPTER 3

PSYCHOANALYTIC THERAPY

Psychoanalytic therapy, rooted in the theories of Sigmund Freud, is a form of verbal therapy aiming to explore the influence of the unconscious mind on thoughts and behaviors. Freud, a pioneer in psychology, founded psychoanalysis to provide insight and resolution for individuals seeking therapy.

What is psychoanalytic therapy?

This therapeutic approach typically delves into the client's early childhood experiences to identify events that may have significantly impacted their life or contributed to current concerns. It is considered a long-term choice, with sessions extending over weeks, months, or even years, depending on the depth of the issues being explored.

How does psychoanalytic therapy operate?

Insight-driven, psychoanalytic therapy fosters change by helping individuals understand their past and its potential impact on their present. Sessions involve open conversations in a safe, non-judgmental environment. The therapist listens for patterns or significant events, emphasizing the belief that unconscious feelings and childhood experiences play a pivotal role in mental distress.

In addition to discussing experiences and concerns, the therapist may employ techniques like free association, therapeutic transference, and interpretation.

Free association: This involves speaking freely about whatever comes to mind without censoring thoughts or memories. The aim is to return to an earlier emotional state, facilitating a better understanding of recurrent patterns of conflict.

Therapeutic transference:

This addresses the transfer of thoughts or feelings related to influential figures in one's life onto the therapist. The therapist discusses transference to help gain insights into interpersonal dynamics.

Interpretation: An integral part of psychoanalytic therapy, interpretation involves the therapist occasionally interjecting with thoughts or interpretations. The therapist may also explore dream analysis, considering dreams as valuable resources for understanding the unconscious.

Applications of psychoanalytic therapy: This form of therapy is suitable for individuals with specific emotional concerns or those seeking self-exploration. It is considered effective for general issues like anxiety, relationship difficulties, sexual concerns, or low self-esteem, but may be less suitable for those seeking quick, solution-focused therapies. Psychoanalytic therapy, whether in individual or group settings, is a gradual process with potentially life-changing results.

Choosing the right counseling: The selection of therapy depends on individual preferences and needs. Researching different types of therapy, seeking advice from professionals, and engaging in discussions with potential counselors can help in making an informed decision. If one type of therapy proves ineffective, communication with the counselor can lead to a collaborative solution. Patience and flexibility are key in finding the most suitable therapeutic approach.

CHAPTER 4

COMMON MENTAL HEALTH DISORDERS

Anxiety Disorders

Anxiety disorders fall under the umbrella of mental health conditions, posing challenges in navigating daily life. Individuals grappling with anxiety may encounter symptoms such as nervousness, panic, fear, sweating, and an accelerated heartbeat. Treatment options encompass medication and cognitive behavioral therapy, with healthcare professionals tailoring a personalized plan for optimal results.

Unraveling the Layers of Mental Health Challenges

Anxiety disorders transcend the ordinary feelings of unease tied to specific situations. For those affected, reactions to triggers may manifest as fear and dread, accompanied by physical manifestations like a racing heart and perspiration. While experiencing occasional anxiety is normal and even beneficial, an anxiety disorder disrupts daily functioning, leading to overreactions and a lack of control in response to stimuli.

Who is Prone to Anxiety Disorders?

Various factors contribute to an individual's susceptibility to anxiety disorders, encompassing a mix of genetics and environmental influences. Risk factors include specific personality traits, exposure to stress or trauma, a family history of mental health conditions, and certain physical ailments like thyroid issues and heart arrhythmias. Women face a higher prevalence of anxiety disorders, a phenomenon still under investigation, possibly linked to hormonal fluctuations and treatment-seeking behaviors.

Exploring Different Anxiety Disorders

An array of anxiety disorders exists, each presenting distinct characteristics:

Generalized Anxiety Disorder (GAD): Persistent and excessive worry about various aspects of life.

Panic Disorder: Recurrent, unexpected panic attacks accompanied by intense fear.

Phobias: Intense fears of specific objects, situations, or activities.

Separation Anxiety: Distress when separated from attachment figures.

Overlap with Other Conditions: Anxiety disorders share features with related mental health conditions like post-traumatic stress disorder and obsessive-compulsive disorder.

Navigating the landscape of anxiety disorders involves recognizing symptoms, understanding risk factors, and embracing tailored treatments to promote mental well-being.

Understanding Generalized Anxiety Disorder (GAD):

Generalized Anxiety Disorder (GAD) is characterized by an overwhelming and unrealistic sense of worry and tension, persisting even in the absence of apparent triggers. Individuals with GAD find themselves preoccupied with concerns related to health, work, school, and relationships on most days. Physical manifestations may include restlessness, difficulty concentrating, and sleep disturbances.

Exploring Panic Disorder: Panic Disorder involves the occurrence of intense and abrupt panic attacks, which often surpass the intensity of other anxiety disorders. These attacks may arise suddenly or be triggered by specific situations, inducing feelings of terror. Symptoms can mimic those of a heart attack, warranting immediate medical attention. Individuals with panic disorder may experience sweating, heart palpitations, chest pain, and a sensation of choking, leading to persistent worries about future attacks and avoidance of triggering situations.

Unraveling Phobias: Phobias entail an intense and irrational fear of particular situations or objects. While some fears may align with common concerns, the intensity of the fear may not correspond to the actual threat. Like other anxiety disorders, individuals with phobias often go to great lengths to avoid situations that trigger their fears. Specific phobias may include fears of animals, blood, flying, heights, and injections.

Social Anxiety Disorder: Formerly known as social phobia, Social Anxiety Disorder manifests as overwhelming worry and self-consciousness in everyday social situations. Individuals fear judgment, embarrassment, or ridicule, often leading to avoidance of social interactions.

Understanding Agoraphobia: Agoraphobia involves an intense fear of being overwhelmed or unable to seek help in specific environments. Fears may encompass enclosed spaces, lines or crowds, open spaces, places outside the home, and public transportation. In severe cases, individuals with agoraphobia may avoid leaving their homes altogether due to the apprehension of experiencing a panic attack in public.

Exploring Separation Anxiety Disorder: While more common in children and teens, Separation Anxiety Disorder can also affect adults who have experienced stressful events. Children with this disorder worry about being away from their parents, fearing harm or non-return. The condition often surfaces in preschoolers but may persist into later years, impacting daily activities and causing reluctance to engage in new experiences.

Prevalence of Anxiety Disorders: Anxiety disorders stand as the most prevalent mental health conditions in the United States, affecting approximately 40 million Americans. Nearly 30% of adults experience anxiety disorders at some point, with onset commonly occurring in childhood, adolescence, or early adulthood.

Impact on Children: While it is normal for children to experience occasional anxiety, persistent and overwhelming fears that interfere with daily activities may indicate an anxiety disorder. Recognizing when a child is stuck on their worries and struggles to function in their routine activities is crucial. Seeking professional help becomes essential when anxiety impedes a child's ability to navigate school, play, and sleep.

Symptoms and Causes of Anxiety Disorders

Anxiety disorders, akin to other mental illnesses, are not attributed to personal weakness, character flaws, or upbringing issues. The precise causes of anxiety disorders remain unclear, with researchers pointing to a likely combination of factors:

Chemical Imbalance: Prolonged or intense stress can alter the chemical balance that regulates mood, potentially leading to the development of an anxiety disorder.

Environmental Factors: Traumatic experiences may act as triggers for anxiety disorders, particularly in individuals with an inherited predisposition.

Heredity: Anxiety disorders tend to have a familial pattern, running in families and having a hereditary component similar to traits like eye color.

Symptoms of Anxiety Disorders

The symptoms of anxiety disorders can vary depending on the specific type. However, general manifestations encompass physical, mental, and behavioral aspects:

Physical Symptoms:

- Cold or sweaty hands
- Dry mouth.
- Heart palpitations.
- Nausea.
- Numbness or tingling in hands or feet.
- Muscle tension.
- Shortness of breath.

Mental Symptoms:

- Feelings of panic, fear, and uneasiness.
- Nightmares.
- Repeated thoughts or flashbacks of traumatic experiences.

- Uncontrollable, obsessive thoughts.

Behavioral Symptoms:

- Inability to be still and calm.
- Ritualistic behaviors, such as repetitive hand washing.
- Trouble sleeping.

Identifying Anxiety in Children:

In children, anxiety-related problems exhibit common features:

- The anxiety is typically a fear or fixation hindering the enjoyment of life, daily functioning, or task completion.
- Both the child and parents find the anxiety puzzling.
- Logical explanations fail to alleviate the worries.
- The anxiety is treatable.

Diagnosis of Anxiety Disorders:

Diagnosing anxiety disorders involves a comprehensive process:

Medical Evaluation: Healthcare providers conduct a thorough medical history and physical examination. While there are no specific lab tests for anxiety disorders, certain tests may be conducted to rule out physical conditions mimicking anxiety symptoms.

Referral to Mental Health Professionals: If no signs of physical illness are identified, providers may refer individuals to psychiatrists or psychologists. These specialists employ interview and assessment tools, considering reported symptoms, daily life interference, and behavioral observations. The Diagnostic and Statistical Manual of Mental Disorders (DSM-5) serves as a standard reference for diagnosing mental illnesses.

Management and treatment of anxiety disorders

Treatment Approaches: Anxiety disorders necessitate professional treatment, acknowledging that they are health issues, not reflections of personal weakness. A comprehensive treatment plan, tailored by healthcare providers, often involves a combination of medication and psychotherapy.

Medication for Anxiety Disorders: While medications cannot cure anxiety disorders, they can alleviate symptoms and enhance daily functioning. Common medications include:

Anti-anxiety medications: Such as benzodiazepines, for short-term relief. Tolerance development may limit long-term effectiveness.

Antidepressants: Addressing brain chemical imbalances to improve mood and reduce stress. Healthcare providers determine the appropriate medication, dosage, and combination, with close monitoring to ensure efficacy and manage potential side effects.

Psychotherapy for Anxiety Disorders: Psychotherapy, particularly Cognitive Behavioral Therapy (CBT), is a key component in managing anxiety disorders. CBT focuses on recognizing and altering thought patterns and behaviors contributing to troublesome feelings. Exposure therapy, involving facing fears and engaging with avoided activities, is also utilized.

Untreated Anxiety Disorders in Children

Neglecting treatment for a child with an anxiety disorder can adversely impact:

- Family relationships.
- School performance.
- Social functioning.

Untreated anxiety may lead to more severe mental and physical health problems. Effective treatment can significantly improve a child's symptoms and overall well-being.

Prevention Strategies: While anxiety disorders cannot be prevented, symptom control and reduction are achievable through:

Medication Caution: Consult healthcare providers before using over-the-counter medications or herbal remedies, as some may exacerbate anxiety symptoms.

Caffeine Limitation: Reduce or eliminate caffeine intake (coffee, tea, cola, chocolate).

Healthy Lifestyle: Maintain regular exercise and a balanced diet.

Seeking Help: Counseling and support following a traumatic event can prevent anxiety from disrupting life.

Outlook for Anxiety Disorders: Properly diagnosed and treated anxiety disorders can significantly enhance the quality of life, relationships, and overall productivity. Combining medications and counseling is often effective in managing symptoms and promoting well-being.

Coping Strategies for Individuals with Anxiety Disorders

Stress Management: Learn stress-reduction techniques, such as meditation.

Support Groups: Engage in in-person or online support groups to share experiences and coping strategies.

Education: Understand the specific type of anxiety disorder to regain control, and educate friends and family for better support.

Caffeine Regulation: Many individuals with anxiety disorders find symptom relief by limiting or avoiding caffeine.

Communication with Healthcare Provider: Regularly communicate with healthcare providers regarding treatment progress, concerns about medication, and overall well-being.

Relationship Between Irritable Bowel Syndrome (IBS) and Anxiety Disorders

IBS and anxiety often coexist, with stress impacting digestive symptoms. Managing stress through psychotherapy and stress management may alleviate IBS symptoms.

Emergency Room Visit for Anxiety Disorders: If anxiety symptoms mimic a heart attack or pose concerns about overall health, seeking emergency care is recommended. Any uncertainty about symptoms warrants a visit to the emergency room, where healthcare professionals can assess and provide necessary treatment.

Questions for Healthcare Provider: Individuals with anxiety disorders should inquire about the following:

Best Treatment Plan: Seek guidance on the most effective treatment approach.

Medication Need and Type: Clarify the necessity and type of medication, along with its duration.

Psychotherapy Options: Discuss the most suitable psychotherapy techniques.

Symptom Management Strategies: Explore additional methods to manage symptoms effectively.

Risk for Other Conditions: Inquire about potential risks for coexisting conditions.

Mood disorders

A mood disorder is a mental health condition that significantly impacts emotional states, leading to prolonged periods of intense happiness, deep sadness, or a combination of both. Some mood disorders may also involve persistent emotions like anger and irritability. While it's natural for moods to fluctuate based on circumstances, a mood disorder diagnosis requires the presence of symptoms lasting several weeks or longer, affecting behavior and daily activities such as work or school.

Common Mood Disorders:

The two most prevalent mood disorders are depression and bipolar disorder. Additionally, other mood disorders include:

Depression and its Subtypes: Depression, also known as major or clinical depression, is characterized by feelings of sadness or hopelessness. Symptoms may impact thinking, memory, eating, and sleeping. Subtypes include postpartum depression, persistent depressive disorder, and seasonal affective disorder.

Bipolar Disorder and its Subtypes: Bipolar disorder involves extreme mood swings, cycling between episodes of mania (elevated mood) and depression. Subtypes include bipolar I disorder, bipolar II disorder, cyclothymic disorder, and other specified and unspecified bipolar disorders.

Premenstrual Dysphoric Disorder: This disorder involves severe mood changes, irritability, and tension occurring in the premenstrual phase of the menstrual cycle.

Disruptive Mood Deregulation Disorder: Primarily diagnosed in children and adolescents, this disorder is characterized by chronic irritability and temper outbursts disproportionate to the situation.

Types of Depression

Several types of depression exist, each with distinct characteristics:

Postpartum Depression (Peripartum Depression): Occurs during or after pregnancy, marked by hormonal, physical, emotional, financial, and social changes.

Persistent Depressive Disorder: A chronic form of depression lasting at least two years, with occasional fluctuations in severity. It is less severe than major depressive disorder but persistent.

Seasonal Affective Disorder (SAD): Depressive episodes linked to specific seasons, commonly beginning in late autumn or early winter and resolving in spring or summer.

Understanding Depression: Depression is a prevalent mental health condition with various types, including postpartum depression, persistent depressive disorder, and seasonal affective disorder. Each subtype has distinct characteristics and durations, emphasizing the need for tailored treatment approaches.

Depression

Depression with psychosis is a severe form of depression accompanied by psychotic episodes, which may involve hallucinations (seeing or hearing things others don't) or delusions (fixed but false beliefs). Individuals with this condition are at an increased risk of contemplating suicide.

Bipolar Disorder

Bipolar disorder is a lifelong mood disorder characterized by intense mood swings, energy level fluctuations, altered thinking patterns, and behavioral changes. There are four primary types of bipolar disorder:

Bipolar I Disorder: Involves one or more manic episodes, often accompanied by depressive episodes.

Bipolar II Disorder: Characterized by cycles of depression and hypomania, a less severe form of mania.

Cyclothymic Disorder (Cyclothymia): Results in chronically unstable mood states with hypomanic and mild depressive periods lasting at least two years.

Other Specified and Unspecified Bipolar and Related Disorders: Includes symptoms not meeting criteria for the other types but still causing significant mood changes.

Other Mood Disorders

Other mood disorders encompass:

Premenstrual Dysphoric Disorder (PMDD): Occurs before menstruation, presenting with severe mood symptoms such

as anger, irritability, anxiety, depression, and
insomnia.

Disruptive Mood Dysregulation Disorder (DMDD):

Affects children and adolescents, involving frequent anger outbursts and irritability disproportionate to situations, surpassing intermittent explosive disorder (IED) in severity.

Is Anxiety a Mood Disorder?

Anxiety, specifically generalized anxiety disorder, is not classified as a mood disorder but falls under the category of anxiety disorders. Despite this distinction, anxiety often coexists with or precedes mood disorders such as depression.

Affected Population: Mood disorders can impact anyone, spanning children, adolescents, and adults. Major depression is more prevalent in women and individuals assigned female at birth (AFAB) compared to men and individuals assigned male at birth (AMAB).

Prevalence of Mood Disorders: Mood disorders are relatively common in adults, with depression and bipolar disorder being the most prevalent. In the United States, approximately 7% of adults experience depression, while around 2.8% grapple with bipolar disorder. Children and adolescents also face mood disorders, with an estimated 15% affected by any mood disorder.

Symptoms of Mood Disorders

General Symptoms: Mood disorders exhibit diverse symptoms affecting mood, sleep, eating habits, energy levels, and cognitive functions, varying across specific disorders. In general:

Depressive Symptoms:

- Persistent sadness.
- Lack of energy or sluggishness.
- Feelings of worthlessness or hopelessness.
- Loss of interest in previously enjoyable activities.
- Thoughts of death or suicide.
- Difficulty concentrating or focusing.
- Sleep disturbances (excessive or insufficient).
- Changes in appetite (overeating or loss of appetite).

Hypomanic or Manic Episode Symptoms:

- Extreme energy or elation.
- Rapid speech or movement.
- Agitation, restlessness, or irritability.
- Risk-taking behavior (e.g., reckless driving, excessive spending).
- Racing thoughts.
- Insomnia or sleep difficulties.

Causes of Mood Disorders

Biological Factors: The amygdala and orbitofrontal cortex, responsible for emotions, may play a role in mood disorders. Brain imaging shows an enlarged amygdala in individuals with mood disorders.

Genetic Factors: A strong family history of mood disorders increases the likelihood of developing such conditions, indicating a genetic/inherited component.

Environmental Factors:

Stressful Life Changes: Events like the loss of a loved one, chronic stress, traumatic experiences, and childhood abuse are significant risk factors, particularly for depression.

 Chronic Illness: Depression is linked to chronic conditions such as diabetes, Parkinson's disease, and heart disease.

Diagnosis of Mood Disorders

If symptoms suggestive of a mood disorder are present, healthcare providers typically follow these diagnostic steps:

Physical Examination: Rule out physiological causes like thyroid disease, other illnesses, or nutritional deficiencies.

Medical History: Inquire about medical history, medications, and family history of mood disorders.

Mental Health Professional Referral: If necessary, referral to a mental health professional for a comprehensive evaluation.

Symptoms of Mood Disorders

General Symptoms: Mood disorders exhibit diverse symptoms affecting mood, sleep, eating habits, energy levels, and cognitive functions, varying across specific disorders. In general:

Depressive Symptoms:

- Persistent sadness.
- Lack of energy or sluggishness.
- Feelings of worthlessness or hopelessness.
- Loss of interest in previously enjoyable activities.
- Thoughts of death or suicide.
- Difficulty concentrating or focusing.
- Sleep disturbances (excessive or insufficient).

- Changes in appetite (overeating or loss of appetite).

Hypomanic or Manic Episode Symptoms:

- Extreme energy or elation.

- Rapid speech or movement.

- Agitation, restlessness, or irritability.

- Risk-taking behavior (e.g., reckless driving, excessive spending).

- Racing thoughts.

- Insomnia or sleep difficulties.

Prevention

Currently, there's no known way to prevent mood disorders. However, early intervention and treatment can help mitigate related issues. Seeking assistance as soon as symptoms manifest can minimize disruptions to daily life.

Outlook / Prognosis:

The prognosis for mood disorders depends on several factors:

- Type and Severity: The specific condition and its severity impact the outlook.
- Early Diagnosis: Early detection contributes to better outcomes.
- Proper Treatment: Appropriate and timely treatment is crucial for a positive prognosis.

Recurrence and Lifelong Treatment

Depression and bipolar disorder may recur or require long-term or lifetime treatment.

Associated Risks:

- About one-third of individuals with a mood disorder develop psychotic disorders, and another one-third develop a lifetime anxiety disorder.
- Increased risk of suicidal behavior, emphasizing the importance of seeking help immediately.

- Elevated risk of disability, missing work or school, severe anxiety, alcohol use disorder, and substance use disorder.

Living With Mood Disorders:

- Mood disorders are treatable, and finding the right treatment plan is crucial.
- Stay committed to feeling better, even if it takes time to identify the most effective approach.

When to See a Healthcare Provider

Experiencing Symptoms: If you or your child are displaying symptoms of a mood disorder, consult a healthcare provider.

Diagnosed with a Mood Disorder

- Regular visits to your provider or mental health professional are essential to monitor and adjust the treatment plan as needed.
- Discuss any concerns, including medication changes or potential side effects, with your

provider for guidance on adjustments or alternative options.

CHAPTER 5

PSYCHOTIC DISORDERS

Psychotic disorders encompass a range of serious mental illnesses that impact cognitive functions, emotional responses, communication, and behavior. Individuals with psychotic disorders often struggle to maintain clarity of thought, make sound judgments, and handle daily life effectively. Despite the severity, these disorders are generally treatable.

Types of Psychotic Disorders

Schizophrenia: Characterized by lasting changes in behavior, delusions, and hallucinations extending beyond six months. It affects various aspects of life, including work, school, and relationships.

Schizoaffective Disorder: Combines symptoms of schizophrenia with a mood disorder like depression or bipolar disorder.

Schizophrenia form Disorder: Exhibits symptoms similar to schizophrenia, but the duration is shorter, typically lasting between 1 and 6 months.

Brief Psychotic Disorder: Involves a sudden, short-lived episode of psychotic behavior, often triggered by intense stress, with recovery usually within a month.

Delusional Disorder: Defined by persistent false beliefs (delusions) related to real-life situations, lasting at least 1 month.

Shared Psychotic Disorder (Folie à Deux): Occurs when one person in a relationship has a delusion, and the other person adopts the same belief.

Substance-Induced Psychotic Disorder: Caused by drug use or withdrawal, leading to hallucinations, delusions, or confused speech.

Psychotic Disorder Due to Another Medical Condition: Hallucinations, delusions, or other symptoms result from an underlying medical condition affecting brain function, such as a head injury or brain tumor.

Understanding and recognizing the specific types of psychotic disorders is crucial for appropriate diagnosis and treatment. Early intervention and comprehensive care can significantly improve outcomes for individuals with these conditions.

Causes and Diagnosis of Psychotic Disorders

Causes:

Genetic Factors: Some psychotic disorders tend to run in families, indicating a partial genetic influence.

Environmental Factors: Stress, drug abuse, and major life changes may contribute to the development of psychotic disorders.

Brain Abnormalities: Individuals with certain psychotic disorders, like schizophrenia, may exhibit problems in brain regions controlling thinking, perception, and motivation.

Neurotransmitter Dysfunction: In conditions like schizophrenia, issues with nerve cell receptors working with the neurotransmitter glutamate may contribute to cognitive and perceptual problems.

Age of Onset: Psychotic disorders typically emerge in late teens, 20s, or 30s and affect men and women equally.

Diagnosis:

Medical and Psychiatric History: Doctors assess a person's history, looking for symptoms and relevant life events.

Physical Exam: A brief physical examination may be conducted to rule out physical illnesses contributing to symptoms.

Blood Tests: Blood tests may be performed to check for underlying medical conditions and rule out drug use.

Brain Imaging: Techniques like MRI scans may be used to examine the brain and exclude physical abnormalities.

Referral to Mental Health Professionals: If physical causes are ruled out, the person may be referred to a psychiatrist or psychologist.

Interviews and Assessment Tools: Mental health professionals use specialized interviews and assessments to determine the presence of a psychotic disorder.

Treatment of Psychotic Disorders

1. Medication

Antipsychotics: Medications primarily prescribed are antipsychotics to manage symptoms like delusions, hallucinations, and cognitive issues.

Older Antipsychotics:

- Chlorpromazine (Thorazine)
- Fluphenazine (Prolixin)
- Haloperidol (Haldol)
- Loxapine (Loxitane)
- Perphenazine (Trilafon)
- Thioridazine (Mellaril)

Newer Atypical Antipsychotics:

- Aripiprazole (Abilify)
- Asenapine (Saphris)
- Brexpiprazole (Rexulti)
- Cariprazine (Vraylar)
- Clozapine (Clozaril)
- Iloperidone (Fanapt)
- Lurasidone (Latuda)
- Olanzapine (Zyprexa)
- Olanzapine/samidorphan (Lybalvi)
- Paliperidone (Invega)
- Paliperidone palmitate (Invega Sustenna, Invega Trinza)
- Quetiapine (Seroquel)
- Risperidone (Risperdal)
- Ziprasidone (Geodon)

2. Psychotherapy (Counseling)

Individual Psychotherapy: One-on-one sessions with a mental health professional to explore thoughts, feelings, and behaviors.

Cognitive Behavioral Therapy (CBT): Structured therapy addressing distorted thought patterns and behaviors associated with psychotic symptoms.

Family Therapy: Involves family members to enhance support and understanding, crucial for managing psychotic disorders.

Social Skills Training: Focuses on improving social interactions and communication skills.

Other Interventions

Hospitalization: In severe cases or during acute episodes, hospitalization may be necessary.

Electroconvulsive Therapy (ECT): For treatment-resistant cases, ECT may be considered.

Rehabilitation Services: Supportive services to enhance daily functioning, vocational skills, and community integration.

Effective management often involves a combination of medication and psychotherapy tailored to individual needs. Ongoing monitoring and adjustments to the treatment plan contribute to improved outcomes for individuals with psychotic disorders.

Substance use disorders

Substance use disorder, a medical condition characterized by compulsive substance use, poses a significant threat to overall health when it hinders day-to-day functioning. This condition can manifest with the misuse of prescription or nonprescription drugs.

Formerly referred to as drug abuse, substance use disorder is also known as addiction, distinct from dependence. The repercussions of substance misuse extend beyond individual well-being and significantly impact public health. In 2017, the Centers for Disease Control and Prevention (CDC) reported over 70,000 deaths in the United States due to overdoses, while approximately 88,000 people succumbed to the consequences of excessive alcohol use annually.

The adverse effects of substance misuse manifest in various public health issues, including drunk and impaired driving, violence, familial stress, and the heightened potential for child abuse and neglect. Additionally, engaging in intravenous drug use with shared or reused needles increases the risk of contracting and transmitting infectious diseases such as HIV and hepatitis.

The American Psychiatric Association (APA) classifies substance use disorder as a brain disease, marked by persistent substance use despite negative consequences. This condition is influenced by a complex interplay of social and biological factors, emphasizing the need for a comprehensive understanding and approach to address its impact on individuals and society.

Risk factors

The information you provided outlines key risk factors for substance misuse and addiction, particularly focusing on genetic predisposition, experiences of abuse or trauma, environmental influences, mental health disorders, and early initiation of substance use. Additionally, you've highlighted specific risk factors for adolescent substance misuse and provided details on depressants, with a focus on alcohol and heroin.

It's crucial to recognize the complex interplay of these factors in understanding and addressing substance use disorders. Substance misuse often stems from a combination of biological, psychological, and social factors.

Biopsychosocial Model: Substance use disorders are often conceptualized using the biopsychosocial model, which considers biological (genetics, neurobiology), psychological (mental health, personality), and social (environment, relationships) factors.

Prevention and Intervention: Recognizing risk factors is essential for prevention efforts. Early intervention and support for individuals with multiple risk factors can be crucial in preventing the progression from substance use to misuse or addiction.

Adolescent Brain Development: Emphasizing the unique vulnerability of adolescent brains is crucial. The prefrontal cortex, responsible for decision-making and impulse control, is not fully developed in adolescents, making them more susceptible to risky behaviors.

Educational Initiatives: Implementing educational programs can help raise awareness about the risks associated with substance use. Targeting both adolescents and adults, these programs can provide information about the consequences of substance misuse and the importance of seeking help.

Treatment Approaches: Understanding the specific effects of substances like alcohol and heroin is vital for designing effective treatment approaches. Treatment may involve a combination of behavioral therapies, counseling, medication-assisted treatment (MAT), and support groups.

Harm Reduction: Incorporating harm reduction strategies, such as needle exchange programs for individuals using heroin, can help minimize the negative health consequences associated with substance use.

Stigma Reduction: Addressing the stigma surrounding substance use disorders is crucial for promoting a more compassionate and understanding approach to individuals struggling with addiction. Stigma can be a barrier to seeking help.

Multidisciplinary Approach: Addressing substance use disorders often requires a multidisciplinary approach involving healthcare professionals, mental health experts, social workers, and community support services.

Stimulants

Stimulants heighten central nervous system (CNS) activity, providing a temporary boost in alertness, energy, or confidence. However, misuse can result in significant risks such as insomnia, cardiovascular issues, and seizures.

Cocaine

Cocaine, a potent substance, is administered through injection, inhalation, or smoking, inducing energetic and euphoric feelings. Commonly referred to as coke, C, crack, snow, flake, and blow, cocaine use raises body temperature, blood pressure, and heart rate. Prolonged and heavy cocaine use can lead to severe consequences, including heart attacks, respiratory failure, strokes, seizures, and even death. In 2018, approximately 5.5 million Americans aged 12 and older reported using cocaine in the past year.

Methamphetamines

Closely related to amphetamines, methamphetamine can be consumed through various methods, including snorting, injection, or smoking. Known as chalk, meth, ice, crystal, glad, speed, and crank, methamphetamine induces long-term wakefulness and increased physical activity, resulting in elevated heart rate, body temperature, and blood pressure. Extended use may lead to mood problems, violent behavior, anxiety, confusion, insomnia, and severe dental issues.

Marijuana

Derived from various parts of the cannabis plant, marijuana can be smoked or ingested through edibles, producing feelings of euphoria, distorted perceptions, and difficulty in problem-solving. Also known as ganja, pot, weed, grass, 420, and trees, an estimated 43.5 million Americans aged 12 and older used marijuana in 2018. Research supports the exploration of marijuana's potential medical benefits for conditions such as glaucoma and chemotherapy side effects.

Club of Drugs

This category encompasses a variety of substances commonly used at dance parties, clubs, and bars, including:

- Gamma hydroxybutyrate (GHB), also known as grievous bodily harm, G, and liquid ecstasy.

- Ketamine, known as K, special K, vitamin K, and cat valium.

- Methylenedioxymethamphetamine (MDMA), also known as ecstasy, X, XTC, adam, clarity, and molly.

- Lysergic acid diethylamide (LSD), also known as acid.

- Flunitrazepam (Rohypnol), also known as R2 or as a roofie, rophie, roche, or forget-me pill.

These drugs can induce feelings of euphoria, detachment, or sedation. Roofies, in particular, have been associated with sexual assaults. The side effects include serious short-term mental health problems like delirium, physical health issues such as rapid heart rate, seizures, dehydration, and, in extreme cases, death. The risks of these side effects increase when mixed with alcohol.

Other substance

Anabolic Steroids: Commonly known as juice, gym candy, pumpers, and stackers, these lab-made substances mimic testosterone and are used orally or through injection. While legal with a prescription in the U.S., athletes may misuse them to enhance performance, leading to serious health problems such as aggressive behavior, liver damage, high blood pressure, high cholesterol, and infertility. Women who misuse steroids may experience additional symptoms like facial hair growth, menstrual cycle changes, baldness, and a deepened voice. Teens who misuse steroids may face impaired growth, accelerated puberty, and severe acne.

Inhalants: Also known as whip-its, poppers, and snappers, inhalants are chemical vapors inhaled to induce mind-altering effects. Common products include glue, hair spray, paint, and lighter fluid. Short-term effects mimic the feeling of alcohol use, but using inhalants comes with risks such as a loss of sensation, consciousness, hearing, spasms, brain damage, and heart failure. In 2018, around 2 million people aged 12 and older reported using inhalants in the past year, representing 0.7 percent of Americans in this age group.

Prescription Drug

Many individuals receive prescriptions to manage pain and other health conditions. Prescription drug misuse occurs when individuals use medication not prescribed to them or for reasons other than those directed by their doctor. Substance use disorders can develop even when medications are taken as prescribed. Some examples of commonly misused prescription drugs include opioids like fentanyl and oxycodone, anxiety or sleep medications such as alprazolam and diazepam, and stimulants like methylphenidate, amphetamine and dextroamphetamine. Misuse can result in various effects, including drowsiness, depressed breathing, slowed brain function, anxiety, paranoia, and seizures. The misuse of prescription drugs has increased over the past few decades, partly due to their increased availability.

Stages of Substance Use Disorder

Experts categorize substance use disorder into stages:

1. Experimental Use: Using the substance with peers for recreation.

2. Regular Use: Changing behavior and using the substance to cope with negative feelings.

3. Daily Preoccupation or Risky Use: Being preoccupied with the substance and neglecting life outside substance use.

4. Dependence: Inability to face life without the substance, leading to increased personal and financial problems, as well as legal issues.

Treating Substance Use Disorder

Medical treatment is available for substance use disorders, following key principles:

- Addiction is a complex but treatable health condition.
- No single treatment works for everyone.

- Treatment should be readily available and address multiple needs.
- Mental health is a crucial aspect of treatment.
- Regular evaluation ensures that treatment meets individual needs.
- Remaining in treatment for an adequate duration is essential.

Treatment may involve individual and group counseling, and medications can be prescribed to ease withdrawal symptoms and aid recovery.

Detoxification

The initial stage of treatment may involve medically assisted detoxification, providing supportive care as substances are cleared from the bloodstream. Detoxification is followed by other treatments, often involving counseling in outpatient or inpatient settings.

Medications can be used to reduce withdrawal symptoms and support recovery.

Preventing Substance Use Disorder

Preventing substance use disorder involves education, safety practices, mental healthcare, community outreach, and reducing stigma. Harm reduction programs can minimize complications of substance use and facilitate access to treatment. For parents concerned about their children's substance use, creating a safe and open space for communication is essential, fostering knowledge and trust.

CHAPTER 6

COGNITIVE-BEHAVIORAL THERAPY (CBT)

Cognitive Behavioral Therapy (CBT) is a form of psychotherapeutic intervention designed to assist individuals in recognizing and modifying destructive or distressing thought patterns that negatively impact their behavior and emotions.

CBT integrates cognitive therapy with behavior therapy by identifying and replacing maladaptive patterns of thinking, emotional responses, and behaviors with more desirable alternatives. The focus of CBT is on altering automatic negative thoughts that contribute to emotional difficulties, depression, and anxiety, thereby influencing mood negatively.

Within the framework of CBT, faulty thoughts are pinpointed, challenged, and substituted with more objective and realistic thoughts. This therapeutic approach encompasses various techniques and methods addressing thoughts, emotions, and behaviors, ranging from structured psychotherapies to self-help practices.

Specific cognitive behavioral therapy approaches include:

Cognitive Therapy: Identifying and altering inaccurate or distorted thought patterns, emotional responses, and behaviors.

Dialectical Behavior Therapy (DBT): Addressing destructive thoughts and behaviors while incorporating strategies like emotional regulation and mindfulness.

Multimodal Therapy: Treating psychological issues by addressing seven interconnected modalities, including behavior, affect, sensation, imagery, cognition, interpersonal factors, and drug-biological considerations.

Rational Emotive Behavior Therapy (REBT): Identifying irrational beliefs, actively challenging them, and learning to recognize and change these thought patterns.

While these approaches differ, they all aim to address the underlying thought patterns contributing to psychological distress.

CBT employs a diverse set of techniques to help individuals overcome maladaptive thought patterns. Some of these techniques include:

Identifying Negative Thoughts: Understanding thoughts, feelings, and situations contributing to maladaptive behaviors.

Practicing New Skills: Learning and practicing new coping skills in real-world situations.

Goal-Setting: Establishing and strengthening goal-setting skills, including setting specific, measurable, attainable, relevant, and time-based (SMART) goals.

Problem-Solving: Developing problem-solving skills to identify and address life stressors.

Self-Monitoring: Tracking behaviors, symptoms, or experiences over time and sharing them with a therapist to inform treatment.

What Cognitive Behavioral Therapy Can Address

Cognitive Behavioral Therapy (CBT) is a versatile short-term treatment designed to guide individuals in focusing on present thoughts and beliefs. It has proven effective in managing various mental health conditions and helping individuals cope with life challenges.

CBT is employed to address a diverse range of conditions, including but not limited to:

- Addiction
- Anger Issues
- Anxiety
- Bipolar Disorder
- Depression
- Eating Disorders
- Panic Attacks
- Personality Disorders
- Phobias

In addition to mental health concerns, CBT has demonstrated efficacy in assisting individuals facing challenges such as:

- Chronic Pain or Serious Illnesses
- Divorce or Break-ups
- Grief or Loss
- Insomnia
- Low Self-esteem
- Relationship Problems
- Stress Management

Benefits of Cognitive Behavioral Therapy

The core principle of CBT is the recognition of the influential role thoughts and feelings play in shaping behavior. For instance, someone consistently dwelling on plane crashes may avoid air travel due to heightened anxiety.

CBT aims to empower individuals by teaching them that, while control over the external world is limited, they can manage how they interpret and respond to their surroundings.

Key benefits of CBT include:

Development of Healthier Thought Patterns: CBT fosters awareness of negative and unrealistic thoughts, leading to the cultivation of healthier thought patterns that positively impact emotions and moods.

Short-Term Effectiveness: Tangible improvements often occur within five to 20 sessions, making it an efficient short-term treatment option.

Versatility: CBT is effective in addressing a wide spectrum of maladaptive behaviors.

Affordability: It is often more cost-effective compared to some other therapeutic approaches.

Adaptability: Whether delivered online or face-to-face, CBT remains effective.

Medication-Free Option: CBT can be employed for individuals who do not require psychotropic medication, providing a non-pharmacological treatment option.

Effectiveness of Cognitive Behavioral Therapy (CBT)

Cognitive Behavioral Therapy (CBT) has a rich history, originating in the 1960s with psychiatrist Aaron Beck's work, identifying the role of certain thought patterns in contributing to emotional issues. Unlike earlier behavior therapies, which focused on external factors, CBT recognizes the impact of thoughts and feelings on behavior.

Key Points on the Effectiveness of CBT:

Extensive Research Base: CBT is one of the most extensively studied forms of treatment. It has demonstrated effectiveness across a range of mental health conditions, including anxiety, depression, eating disorders, insomnia, obsessive-compulsive disorder, panic disorder, post-traumatic stress disorder, and substance use disorders.

Evidence-Based Treatment for Eating Disorders: Research highlights CBT as the leading evidence-based treatment for eating disorders.

Insomnia and Sleep Disorders: CBT has proven helpful for individuals with insomnia and those with medical conditions affecting sleep, such as pain or mood disorders like depression.

Children and Adolescents: Scientific evidence supports the efficacy of CBT in treating symptoms of depression and anxiety in children and adolescents.

Anxiety-Related Disorders: Meta-analyses have shown that CBT is effective in improving symptoms in anxiety-related disorders, including obsessive-compulsive disorder and post-traumatic stress disorder.

Substance Use Disorders: CBT is empirically supported in the treatment of substance use disorders, aiding individuals in improving self-control, avoiding triggers, and developing coping mechanisms for daily stressors.

Measurable Results: CBT's focus on specific goals and measurable outcomes contributes to its extensive research, making it one of the most researched therapy types.

Positive Perception by Clients: According to Very well Mind's Cost of Therapy Survey, a significant majority of individuals find therapy to be a worthwhile investment, expressing satisfaction with the quality of therapy received and progress toward mental health goals.

Challenges and Considerations:

Change Difficulty: Some individuals may find it challenging to change despite recognizing irrational or unhealthy thoughts.

Structured Nature: CBT's structured approach may not be suitable for those who struggle with structured interventions or have a preference for more open-ended therapy.

Readiness for Change: Successful CBT outcomes depend on an individual's readiness and willingness to invest time and effort in self-analysis.

Gradual Progress: CBT is often a gradual process, involving incremental steps towards behavior change. This approach helps individuals make progress by breaking down larger goals into manageable steps.

Getting Started With Cognitive Behavioral Therapy (CBT)

If you are considering Cognitive Behavioral Therapy as a treatment option for psychological issues, follow these steps to initiate the process:

Consult with Your Physician: Begin by consulting with your physician to discuss the possibility of CBT as a treatment choice. Check the directory of certified therapists provided by the National Association of Cognitive-Behavioral Therapists to find licensed professionals in your area. Search online for cognitive behavioral therapy near me to locate local therapists specializing in CBT.

Consider Personal Preferences: Evaluate your personal preferences, including whether face-to-face or online therapy is more suitable for you.

Check Health Insurance Coverage: Contact your health insurance provider to determine if CBT is covered, and if so, inquire about the number of sessions covered per year.

Schedule an Appointment: Make an appointment with the chosen therapist, mark it on your calendar, and ensure you prioritize the commitment.

Prepare for Your First Session: Approach your first session with an open mind and a positive attitude. Be prepared to start identifying thoughts and behaviors that may be hindering your progress. Commit to learning and applying strategies to propel yourself forward.

What to Expect During Cognitive Behavioral Therapy:

First Session Similarities: The first session may resemble an initial appointment with any healthcare provider. You may spend time filling out paperwork, including privacy forms, insurance information, medical history, current medications, and a therapist-patient service agreement. Online therapy may involve completing these forms electronically.

Understanding Your Situation: Once the therapist has a comprehensive understanding of your identity, challenges, and therapy goals, the focus will shift to increasing awareness of unhelpful or unrealistic thoughts and beliefs.

Developing Healthier Patterns: Strategies will be implemented to help you develop healthier thought and behavior patterns. Subsequent sessions involve discussions on the effectiveness of implemented strategies, with adjustments made as needed.

Involvement in Techniques: The therapist may suggest CBT techniques for you to practice between sessions, such as journaling to identify negative thoughts or engaging in activities to overcome anxiety.

Approaching CBT with an open mind and actively participating in the therapeutic process enhances the likelihood of successful outcomes. Regular communication with your therapist, commitment to the process, and the application of learned strategies in daily life contribute to the effectiveness of Cognitive Behavioral Therapy.

CHAPTER 7

CBT TECHNIQUES FOR BETTER MENTAL HEALTH

The core principle of Cognitive Behavioral Therapy (CBT) is that your thought patterns influence your emotions, which, in turn, impact your behaviors. Negative thoughts can lead to negative feelings and actions, while reframing these thoughts in a positive way can result in more positive feelings and constructive behaviors. The skills learned in CBT are practical and can be applied throughout your life.

Key aspects of CBT include:

Identifying Problems and Unproductive Thought Patterns: Recognizing specific problems or issues in your daily life. Becoming aware of unproductive thought patterns and understanding their impact.

Reshaping Negative Thinking: Identifying negative thinking and learning to reshape it in a way that changes how you feel.

Learning New Behaviors: Acquiring new behaviors and implementing them in practice.

Therapists may employ various CBT strategies based on your specific issues and goals. Common techniques include:

Cognitive Restructuring or Reframing: Examining negative thought patterns and learning to reframe them positively. Example: Transforming I'm totally useless because I blew the report to the report wasn't my best work, but I'm a valuable employee who contributes in many ways.

Guided Discovery: Therapist understanding your viewpoint and asking questions to challenge beliefs and broaden thinking. Encouraging consideration of evidence supporting and contradicting assumptions.

Exposure Therapy: Gradual exposure to fears or phobias, with guidance on coping strategies. Small increments of exposure can increase confidence in coping abilities.

Journaling and Thought Records: Listing negative thoughts and positive alternatives between sessions. Tracking new thoughts and behaviors since the last session to gauge progress.

Activity Scheduling and Behavior Activation: Placing avoided or delayed activities on a schedule to reduce decision burden. Establishing good habits through activity scheduling and providing opportunities to apply learned skills.

Behavioral Experiments: Primarily used for anxiety disorders with catastrophic thinking. Predicting outcomes before anxiety-inducing tasks and assessing the accuracy of predictions. Gradual exposure to tasks, demonstrating that predicted catastrophes are unlikely to occur.

Relaxation and Stress Reduction Techniques: Progressive relaxation techniques, including deep breathing exercises, muscle relaxation, and imagery. Practical skills to lower stress and enhance control, beneficial for phobias, social anxieties, and various stressors.

Role Playing: Working through behaviors in challenging situations through role playing. Useful for improving problem-solving skills, building familiarity and confidence in certain situations, practicing social skills, assertiveness training, and enhancing communication skills.

Successive Approximation: Breaking overwhelming tasks into smaller, achievable steps. Building confidence incrementally as each step builds upon the previous ones.

Applications of CBT:

CBT is versatile and can address a range of everyday problems, such as coping with stress or managing anxiety. It does not require a medical diagnosis and can help with:

Emotion Management: Coping with powerful emotions like anger, fear, or sadness.

Grief: Assisting individuals in dealing with grief.

Symptom Management and Prevention: Managing symptoms and preventing relapses of mental illnesses.

Physical Health Problems: Coping with the psychological aspects of physical health problems.

Conflict Resolution and Communication: Improving conflict resolution skills and enhancing communication skills.

CBT is effective for various conditions, either as a standalone treatment or in combination with other therapies or medications, including:

- Addictions
- Anxiety Disorders
- Bipolar Disorders
- Chronic Pain
- Depression
- Eating Disorders
- Obsessive-Compulsive Disorder (OCD)
- Phobias
- Post-Traumatic Stress Disorder (PTSD)
- Schizophrenia
- Sexual Disorders
- Sleep Disorders
- Tinnitus

Risks and Considerations:

- CBT is generally not considered risky, but individuals may find it stressful initially.

- Some types, like exposure therapy, may temporarily increase stress and anxiety.
- It requires commitment and ongoing practice of techniques between sessions and after therapy concludes.
- CBT is a gradual process, requiring a lifestyle change and ongoing improvement throughout life.

CHAPTER 8

CHILD AND ADOLESCENT PSYCHIATRY

Adolescence involves traversing the delicate bridge between childhood and adulthood, often called the age of risk due to its impact on brain development, stress levels, and susceptibility to depression.

While developmental disorders are relatively uncommon, they are not rare in the realm of children and adolescents. Regardless of the root cause, early diagnosis and appropriate treatment offer substantial advantages. The realm of child and adolescent psychiatry strives to enhance the well-being of young individuals and their families through a blend of medical, educational, social-psychological, and psychotherapeutic interventions.

Child and Adolescent Psychiatry:

Child and adolescent psychiatry, also known as child psychiatry or pediatric psychiatry, is a specialized branch of medicine devoted to identifying and addressing mental health disorders in youngsters and their families. This field encompasses the social, emotional, behavioral, learning, and mental health challenges unique to the developmental phases of childhood and adolescence.

Within this domain, child psychiatrists, who are medical doctors with specialized training, play a crucial role. They undergo extensive training in diagnosing and treating a spectrum of emotional, behavioral, developmental, and social issues in children. Additionally, child psychiatrists engage in research to comprehend the causes, prevention, treatment, and early detection of mental health problems in children. Outreach and education initiatives to enhance childhood mental health care also fall within their purview.

The job of a Child Psychiatrist: Also referred to as pediatric psychiatry, child psychiatry is the domain where medical doctors, specializing in children and adolescents, excel in diagnosing, treating, and preventing mental disorders.

Child psychiatrists conduct assessments and offer treatments for various emotional, behavioral, and developmental challenges, encompassing depression, anxiety, bipolar disorder, ADHD, substance abuse, and autism spectrum disorders. Beyond addressing mental health issues, they tackle problems that impact physical health, such as eating disorders, anxiety disorders, and post-traumatic stress disorder (PTSD).

Apart from prescribing medications, child psychiatrists collaborate with therapists to assist children in navigating life's challenges. They engage in therapeutic conversations, helping children express their emotions and cultivate positive coping mechanisms and social skills.

Navigating the Challenges: Childhood and adolescence mark a period of profound transition, where acquiring new skills, exploring the world, and mastering social interactions are paramount. However, for some, these phases pose difficulties that hinder learning and socializing in various settings. Others grapple with more severe mental health conditions affecting their daily lives.

Statistics from 2015 suggest that around 10% of children aged 6-17 were diagnosed with a mental health condition, as per the National Institute of Mental Health (NIMH). Although this figure may seem substantial, it reflects a lower estimation compared to previous counts, owing to more stringent diagnostic criteria employed today.

Common Child and Adolescent Psychiatric Conditions

The spectrum of psychiatric conditions affecting children and adolescents encompasses:

- ADHD
- Obsessive-compulsive disorder (OCD)
- Conduct disorder (CD)
- Anxiety
- Depression
- Tourette syndrome
- Post-traumatic stress disorder (PTSD)
- Oppositional defiant disorder (ODD)
- Learning Disorders

Searching for a Child or Adolescent Psychiatrist

Psychiatrists, equipped to diagnose and treat mental health disorders, often cater to both adults and children, albeit with varying levels of experience in each demographic. Finding a suitable child or adolescent psychiatrist involves considering several factors. To locate one:

- Seek a referral or recommendation from your child's pediatrician or primary care physician.
- Utilize the Child and Adolescent Psychiatrist Finder on the American Academy of Child and Adolescent Psychiatry's (AACAP) website.
- Explore community health clinics in your area for free or low-cost services.
- Refer to the National Association of Free & Charitable Clinics site.
- Filter through the American Psychiatric Association's database for child and adolescent psychiatrists.

Considering Therapy for Your Child

Therapy can be a valuable avenue for children, providing a space to process emotions and develop coping skills to navigate current stressors. Parents can learn strategies to support their children outside of therapy, contributing to symptom improvement.

Understanding Counseling Duration: The frequency and duration of counseling are unique to each individual, contingent on the intensity of symptoms and underlying concerns. As therapy progresses and symptoms alleviate, sessions may gradually decrease until the child no longer requires counseling.

Addressing Concerns about Psychiatric Medications: Not all psychiatric medications pose a risk of addiction. Effective medication management considers this concern, with patient and doctor collaborating to find the right balance. Regular monitoring tracks progress over time.

Seeking Professional Guidance: Whether your child grapples with emotional or mental challenges or if you have an adolescent asking identity questions, consulting a pediatric psychiatry specialist can yield significant benefits. Even if you're unsure about the need for psychiatric intervention, scheduling an appointment provides an opportunity to explore potential treatment options and gain a deeper understanding of your child's well-being.

CHAPTER 9

GERIATRIC PSYCHIATRY

Geriatric Psychiatry (GPsy) involves providing psychiatric care to older adults, typically those aged 65 and above (Medicare-eligible). Geriatric Psychiatrists (GPts) undergo additional training, extending beyond the standard four-year adult psychiatry residency, with additional qualifications from the American Board of Psychiatry and Neurology in Geriatric Psychiatry. They specialize in addressing late-life psychiatric conditions such as delirium, dementias, depression, mood disorders, anxiety disorders, psychoses, alcohol and substance abuse, personality disorders, and various bio-psycho-social issues specific to the elderly. GPsy fellowships also cover training in psychotherapy for older adults and their families, as well as long-term care psychiatry and consultation liaison. Notably, Geriatric

Psychiatrists excel in managing older adults with multiple coexisting medical conditions and extensive medication regimens, requiring additional training in geriatric medicine and neurology.

Emergence of Geriatric Psychiatry:

Geriatric Psychiatry is a relatively recent specialty in American medicine, with the American Association for Geriatric Psychiatry (AAGP) founded in 1978. The first added qualifications in GPsy exams were introduced in 1991, requiring mandatory recertification every 10 years. The Association of Directors of Geriatric Academic Programs (ADGAP), established in the early 1990s, has played a crucial role in developing a database of GPsy resources and projected needs for the U.S. According to ADGAP statistics, as of 2009, there were 20 million Americans aged over 75, and it was estimated that a minimum of five Geriatric Psychiatrists per 10,000 population over the age of 75 were needed. However, the actual U.S. ratio at that time was only 0.9 per 10,000. Despite having 60 ACGME accredited GPsy programs in 2008, offering 136 spots, only 60 were filled. As of March 2009, there were 1,773 physicians certified in GPsy in the U.S.

The first Division of Geriatric Psychiatry in Missouri began in 1979 at Saint Louis University School of Medicine. In 1993, GPsy fellowship training commenced with a grant from the National Institutes for Mental Health, making it the sixth program funded in the U.S. The Division currently trains three fellows annually in GPsy, requiring prior completion of an adult psychiatry residency. Missouri's Division achieved several milestones, including the creation of a specialized GPsy inpatient unit in 1980, the establishment of the Alzheimer's Disease Community Brain Bank in 1985, and the Saint Louis University Center for Healthy Brain

Aging in 2009, along with the recent development of a late-life mood and anxiety disorders program.

Psychogeriatric Syndromes - Delirium:

Delirium, or acute confusion, is a prevalent condition addressed by GPys, with estimated prevalences ranging from 10% to 60% among older adults in acute care settings and about 0.5% among non-demented elders in the community. The diagnosis of delirium has improved with the use of tools like the Confusion Assessment Method (CAM), which screens for acute onset, inattention, disorganized thinking, altered consciousness, disorientation, memory impairment, perceptual disturbances, and psychomotor agitation or retardation. Delirium is characterized by difficulty focusing and maintaining attention, and its major risk factors include advanced age, pre-existing cognitive impairment, drugs (e.g., anticholinergics, benzodiazepines), and infections (urinary tract and upper respiratory).

Treatment of delirium involves identifying and addressing the underlying cause or trigger. The behavioral and psychiatric concomitants, such as agitation and psychosis, can be challenging to manage until the cause is identified. Minimizing the use of psychotropics and prioritizing environmental-behavioral interventions, like providing a calm environment, soothing music, touch, aromas, and the presence of familiar faces, are recent trends in managing psychiatric symptoms. In cases of acute, uncontrollable behavior, newer antipsychotics or non-anticholinergic drugs like haloperidol may be warranted, with the immediate goal of preventing harm to the patient or others. The use of benzodiazepines is less optimal due to their potential to worsen confusion and cause balance problems and falls.

Dementia

Geriatric Psychiatrists (GPts) play a unique role in the field of medicine by offering assistance to dementia patients and their families/caregivers throughout every stage of the disease. GPts specialize in diagnosing and differentially diagnosing complex dementias, including Lewy-Body dementia, fronto-temporal dementia, and Parkinson's disease dementia, as well as more common disorders like Alzheimer's Disease (AD). Older adults concerned about cognitive decline may consult a GPsy to determine whether their experiences are indicative of normal aging, cognitive changes related to depression, or other treatable conditions. Mild cognitive impairment (MCI) may serve as a precursor to AD or early signs of a progressive dementia.

Alzheimer's Disease stands out as the most prevalent cause of progressive dementia among older adults, with over five million

Americans currently affected, according to estimates from the Alzheimer's Association. Advanced age is the primary risk factor for AD, and with the aging population, there is a projected doubling of AD cases by 2030. Early detection of AD is emphasized for both physicians and patients.

Dementia Treatment

A significant number of treatments for AD, nearly 260, are currently in clinical trials, surpassing those for any other disease except cancer. Ongoing research suggests that existing therapies, such as cholinesterase inhibitors and the NMDA-receptor antagonist memantine, may enhance or stabilize cognition, behavior, and daily activities in some AD patients. Combining these two classes of drugs may potentially delay nursing home placement. Present therapies are considered symptomatic, but future treatments aim to modify the disease itself.

Many of these involve amyloid modulating compounds, including immunotherapies. Advanced clinical trials are exploring monoclonal antibody infusions targeting A-Beta and intravenous immunoglobulin for early AD, while an AD vaccine is also under investigation.

Geriatric Psychiatry is actively involved in the development of new AD treatments and enhancing the understanding and management of behavioral and psychological symptoms of dementias (BPSD), such as those associated with AD. It is noted that symptoms like agitation in AD may not respond as effectively to neuroleptics as previously believed, and there is a black-box warning regarding the use of antipsychotics in dementia patients due to an increased risk of mortality. Current recommendations for BPSD prioritize behavioral and environmental interventions, with antipsychotics reserved for emergency situations involving out-of-control patients where safety is a primary concern. Antidepressants may be considered if depression in the context of dementia is suspected, and anticonvulsants/mood-stabilizers like divalproex and oxcarbazepine might also be useful.

Depression & Anxiety Disorders

Depression poses a significant challenge for older adults, particularly those in hospitals, outpatient settings, and nursing homes, where approximately 20–25% of residents may experience depression. Older adults exhibit double the suicide rate compared to the general population and have an increased prevalence of psychotic and catatonic depression. The latter condition, where severely depressed older adults cease eating and drinking, becoming cachectic, may necessitate urgent psychiatric-medical intervention, often involving electro-convulsive therapy (ECT).

Geriatric Psychiatrists are frequently called upon to address severe depression in elders, treatment-resistant cases, or instances of active suicidality. Newer antidepressants prove beneficial for clinically significant depression in the elderly, while Cognitive-Behavioral Therapy (CBT) may be effective in non-severe cases, especially when the patient is cognitively intact and motivated. In urgent situations, or when antidepressants are not tolerated or treatment-resistant, ECT can be a safe, rapidly effective, and potentially life-saving intervention. Other modalities like Transcranial Magnetic Stimulation (TMS), Vagal Nerve Stimulation (VNS), and even Deep Brain Stimulation (DBS) may be considered for truly treatment-resistant cases. The Saint Louis University Late-life Mood and Anxiety Disorders program offers a comprehensive range of these interventions, including pharmacotherapy, CBT, and neuromodulation.

An emerging concern for Geriatric Psychiatry is Bipolar Affective Disorder (BAD) in the elderly. Typically onset in the second or third decade of life, BAD tends to worsen with advanced age. Older bipolar patients may experience rapid cycling between mania and depression in days to weeks, unlike the typical months or years seen in younger patients. Unfortunately, many older bipolar patients do not tolerate standard medications such as lithium, which is a mainstay among younger individuals with BAD. The trend towards more late-life bipolar admissions is expected to continue, as BAD does not ameliorate with advancing age.

Late-life onset anxiety disorders are relatively rare; however, anxiety symptoms become more prevalent in older adults, often associated with medical conditions, stress, or the loss of loved ones. Generalized Anxiety Disorder (GAD) is the most common anxiety disorder in later life, affecting 5–10% of individuals. Short-acting benzodiazepines are typically used for acute anxiety treatment, but caution is necessary when administering these drugs to older patients. Long-term treatment often involves serotonergic antidepressants. Psychotherapy, particularly Cognitive-Behavioral Therapy (CBT), proves beneficial for motivated, cognitively intact elders. Supportive and interpersonal psychotherapy may effectively address anxiety symptoms related to loss and stress. An emerging concern in older adults is Post-Traumatic Stress Disorder (PTSD), observed in World War II and Vietnam War veterans.

Other Syndromes

Geriatric Psychiatrists frequently assess older adults experiencing sleep disturbances, pain syndromes, personality disorders, and issues related to alcohol and substance abuse. They work closely with families navigating end-of-life issues with elderly loved ones, providing education about palliative care and the roles of hospice and spirituality. This holistic approach underscores the comprehensive role of Geriatric Psychiatry in addressing the diverse needs of older adults.

CONCLUSION

This comprehensive guide surpass the confines of traditional self-help literature, offering a holistic approach to mental well-being. The book blends clinical expertise with compassionate insight, providing a roadmap for individuals seeking understanding, healing, and personal growth.

Structured with care, the book provides various therapeutic modalities, weaving together theory and practical exercises. It not only demystifies the complexities of mental health but also serves as a light of hope for those navigating the intricacies of the human mind.

Psychiatrist's Therapy Book is more than just a guide; it's a companion on the journey to self-discovery. From the importance of self-compassion to the transformative potential of therapeutic relationships, the book encourages readers to view mental health as an ongoing, dynamic exploration. The readers are equipped with practical tools, a deeper understanding of their mental landscape, and the resilience to navigate life's challenges. This empowering volume not only advocates for individual well-being but also envisions a society that embraces mental health as a shared responsibility, free from stigma and judgment.

www.ingramcontent.com/pod-product-compliance
Lightning Source LLC
Chambersburg PA
CBHW050825260726
48660CB00004B/1609